UNKNOCKABLE!

By Choice Not By Force

JODYMAKC

CONTENTS

1

Have A Purpose For Her.

Will she be your asset or liability? This should be self-explanatory with most men but it is not. That is why it is number one on my list. For example, most men tend to see a woman that they are physically attracted to, approach her, get her number, then do and say a bunch of BS like tell lame lies, to hating on another man she is involved with, to flashing money, to you name it (in that order). There is almost no limit as to what most men like this will do for just one thing; and that is get some pussy.

Most men will do and say almost anything that they think will impress the woman that they are attracted to in order to get whatever it is that they want from her. Maybe this is human nature, but the problem is when it is done without a purpose it will not end well 9 times out of ten. "How you start with her, that is how you will end with her". If all you want from her is sex and you will say and do almost anything in order to get it then what will happen once you get it? For this reason, it is vital for someone who wants to get the most out of her to have a clear purpose for her to be in their life. Remember, she will either be a man's asset or liability.

2

Give Her A Proper Interview.

Right after you understand your purpose for her the next thing on this list to do is to give her a proper interview to get a sense of if she is even qualified to converse with you in the first place, let alone be a part of your life, family, or team. Any man that has experience and has been involved with several women and isn't a flat out sucker for women knows that women are no different from men in regards to being on BS and lying. And in a lot of situations and circumstances they are worse than men. These same men will not hesitate to tell you that they wish they never met her or them, let alone loved them.

There are far too many women out here that are nothing more than beautiful sexy pieces of shit (and that is putting it nicely) that is waiting to fuck up the next man's life and then blame him for it. But guess what? In most cases they are right in a way because these men should have never taken it farther than an interview with her and now they regret it.

The main purpose for the interview should be to expose her flaws by asking direct and indirect questions as well as to see if she may be an asset or a liability in your life and future. Not all men have the same plans and goals in life so not all men will have the same purpose for women and because not all men have the same purpose for women, not all of the interviews will have the same questions. Each man's interview should contain the questions that he not only want to know but also NEED know (which is a huge difference because what are her favorite panties is not as important as what is her FICO score or how come ALL of the men in her life ended up having to put his hands on her (hint). Either way, make the questions count and ask as many as you need too!

3

Give Her Clear And Proper Instructions ASAP To Make Sure She Is For You.

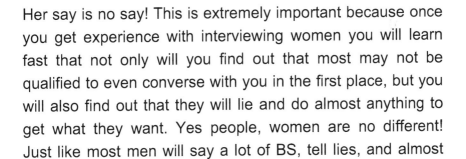

Her say is no say! This is extremely important because once you get experience with interviewing women you will learn fast that not only will you find out that most may not be qualified to even converse with you in the first place, but you will also find out that they will lie and do almost anything to get what they want. Yes people, women are no different! Just like most men will say a lot of BS, tell lies, and almost do anything LITERALLY in order to get what it is that he wants from her; women will also do the same thing.

For this reason it is extremely important to not skip this step because otherwise you will only be taking her word for who she says that she is and what she says that she is about. And even if she has a record for being down for one man doesn't mean that she will be down for you. Think of the interview process as a real job interview so let's use a real job interview for example. We all know people that do this, have done it, or we have done it ourselves. Apply for a job we really want or feel like we need, they call us for an interview, ask us a bunch of questions, we tell them whatever we think they want to hear (it's either a flat out lie or a dramatized truth. Hell, we would even "look" whatever way that helps us get the job.) and a lot of people that need the job will turn into an actor or actress and sincerely give a BS sob story to play on their emotions.

Now, the person on the interview gives her or him a chance because they either like her or feel sorry for her. Then tell them how many hours they will be working, how much they will make starting out, all the benefits, and even will give them a "walk through" to show them the work environment and what they will be doing. After that, they confirm that they are ok with the pay, the hours, and conditions, etc. And guess what? They will say that they are 9 times out of 10. They get hired, start working, get paid, and then start complaining about the exact hours and pay that they agreed to work for and some people beg and cry for. Soon afterwards they quit or got fired because the job put them to work. They had to back all that talking up and they couldn't. They will say that their job is some BS but in reality they are the ones that tried to BS the job.

You can not take her work for it or else you are putting your future in her hands. After you interview her and she passes and you feel good about her, now it is time for her to put her best foot forward by you. It is game time! Put her ass to the test!

To do this, you must give her clear and proper instructions. This is her "training phase" and "probation" phase to see what she is about so make sure that the instructions are clear and accurate. You will not know if she is for you if you do not do this. Most people find out years later after the kids, child support, divorce, etc. that she was never for him because they didn't make sure that she was at the beginning. To make sure that she is, give her clear and proper instructions ASAP. Remember, PROPER INSTRUCTIONS PRODUCES PROPER PROD UCTIONS!

4

Take Your Time With Her.

I like to call this step the "probation phase". This step is crucial because you do not want to prematurely do anything with her, especially if you take your life seriously and want to get the most out of your relationship with her. Every woman that you take seriously should go through the probation phase because while you are in the process of giving her clear and proper instructions to make sure that she is for you, the probation phase is basically allowing yourself time to get to know her for who she actually is and not for who she wants to be.

While on probation, you are giving yourself time to see the results of the instructions that you have given her (or see how she will handle the instructions), give yourself time to capture her mind (which we will look at in the next step), and learn what you need to learn about her in order to stay 2 steps ahead of her (which is an ongoing process and we will look more into in step #6). Personally, 60 to 90 days is usually an ideal probation period for my program.

During this time, through a series of instructions and getting to know her better I usually find out what I need to know in order to make an accurate decision to either make her officially a part of the family or keep her on probation until I'm comfortable. It is not wise to make it official with her before this process. Depending on the man's purpose, program, and system (which will most likely be different from person to person), the probation period may be different. Some shorter, some longer. It should be as long as it takes for you to feel comfortable to make an accurate decision. She will keep asking you and some of the time, pressure you, to make it official but take your time. If you skip this step and rush into it with her because she did a few things for you that made you feel special then you most likely will regret it later. If you don't believe me then ask around, just don't ask a clown!

5

Capture Her Mind.

This step alone can be an entire book or at least an entire article in itself but I will try to sum it up as best as I can. I don't have to remind someone that is capable of pulling this step off how important that it is. If you can control her mind then you can control her body! If you can change the way that she sees things then you will also change the way that she does things! You should work on capturing her mind during the probation process and that includes a basic understanding and appreciation of psychology. Capturing her mind is basically the first process in making her YOURS. Once you have it, she will not believe that she can live without you. To her, you are everything and all that she needs. You can not be replaced, etc. This step may seem difficult to pull off for those that do not have confidence but it is actually easier than you think. In fact, all of these steps are ultimately a part of the process.

The good news is that women are no were near as difficult on a subtle level as they are on the surface. Mainly because women are naturally subtle beings. They operate naturally on a subtle level, men do not. For them "it's the thought that counts" or the time you put into it or the sentimental stuff that you do that makes all the difference in the world to them.

Women are naturally emotional so they will connect emotions to almost anything that you do for them or with them. You must be willing to do things on a subtle level in order to get and keep her mind. They live there! They understand that! If you try to bring her to your world and operate there then you will confuse her and that is when the smallest and simplest shit to us becomes extremely complicated to them. I will give you more examples on how to do this in step 9.

6

Stay 2 Steps Ahead Of Her.

In order to do this you must first know things about her and what she already knows, don't know, and wants to know. This is something that will be an ongoing process as long as she is in your life (if you are doing your job anyways).

No question about it, every real woman no matter how strong they are, aggressive they are, dominant they are, etc. Every woman alive wants to know that she is involved with a man that she respects and can take charge and take the lead and there are men out here for her and she has options (that's if she is "into men"). But you cannot lead her, guide her, or direct her if she knows just as much if not more than you do.

How can you be her knight in shining armor or the answers to all of her questions and problems (which we cover in step 8)? This is why during the probation phase you want to start getting to know her ASAP and not wait until later. Because trust me, they will try to make you wait (for literally NOTHING if you listen to her). Yes it is a job and it is also your future at stake when dealing with these women. It is in her nature to run circles around a sucker and she will do it whether she is conscious of it or not. All ducks MUST get plucked one way or the other. So do yourself a favor and be the King that she needs and not the sucker that she wants by staying two steps ahead of her.

7

Do What You Say That You Will Do.

I can not think of too many things that will turn a woman off faster than her realizing that she was tricked into being involved with a lying fake ass motherfucker who is not about what he says that he is about. It's actually weird because women hate being lied to yet at the same time most are addicted to it. It's almost like they naturally love hearing lies and telling lies.

A lot of men lie and pretend with these women as a tactic to get them because it actually works. Like literally, it actually works. Just tell her what she wants to hear and in most cases you will get the girl. Tell her the truth and keep it real with her then in most cases you will not get the girl. The problem is that you should understand by now that 9 women out of 10 most likely isn't even qualified to converse with you let alone be a part of your life and Future.

If she had it her way you would be her sucker, her puppet, her flunky, or kissing her ass and worshipping her (for absolutely no reason at all). It's quality over quantity. You want that 1% not the 99%. Don't degrade yourself by lying to her or pretending to be someone that you are not just to get her OR keep her. Don't forget that you are the King and the chosen one! Once you get the quality woman or women that you are looking for (and you will) then do what you say that you will do and be who you say that you are.

8

Be The Answers Or Get The Answers To All Of Her Questions And Problems.

A part of being the man of her dreams means that you should also be her go-to person first for any issues or problems that she may have and will have in life. Many times you will not have the answers but that is when you should get the answers for her. It's important that you are someone that she can rely on, depend on, and count on. I mean let's be real about it, you have to give her a valid reason for her to truly believe that she cannot live without you. Just running your mouth in a slick way won't cut it champ! This step is the master key to capturing her mind. If she has to constantly contact or go through another man to handle issues for her then you are not the man of her dreams, don't let her convince you that you are like you are a sucker!

9

Show Her That You Appreciate Her.

Everyone wants to know that they are appreciated by someone that they are involved with. This step is so powerful that it could be the difference between her constantly going all out for you and her barely wanting to do anything for you or with you at all. Yet so simple anyone can do it literally.

I call showing appreciation a reward because that is how I personally use it. I reward her when she is doing good by doing certain things for her or with her that shows her that I appreciate her. A lot of times it takes being creative and sometimes it doesn't. You definitely don't want to do the same thing over and over again because after so long they often get used to it and take it for granted. Some women are not as difficult to please as others.

For example, while learning more about her you find out that she is extremely family oriented and close to her siblings, mother, and father but has never met her grandparents and wishes like hell she did. A great way to reward her is to look up her family tree or something like ancestry DNA and take her to where her roots start. But even doing something very special for her family is another way.

Another one is a woman that isn't used to a guy showing his appreciation for her at all. She is used to not feeling appreciated and used to seeing all of her friends happy in their situations... For them, just send them a $30 basket of roses and a card to work or their house and remind them how much you appreciate her and the kind of woman that she is and how grateful you are to have met her.

(WARNING... be very careful when doing things like this to certain kinds of women. Remember that after a certain point they will really believe that they cannot live without you. Because they are not used to being appreciated, they will not know how to respond to it in most cases and that's when you bring out the crazy in her. And trust me you don't want to see the crazy side of her, and trust me, you don't want to see the crazy side of her, it could be anything from her getting extremely possessive, to her calling the cops lying on you, to her even literally killing you. You have to be careful with doing certain shit for certain kinds of women.)

Another one is a woman that is used to always cooking and taking care of others. Cooking a five-star quality meal with wine and rose petals for her to show her your appreciation is a great way for this type. Women love to eat just as much as men and love being pampered just as much as men. Basically, anything that they love you do or get (well almost anything). And remember, during this step it is supposed to be a reward as your appreciation. A treat from you to them and should ONLY be done when they genuinely deserve it and not just because you like her (which is a huge difference) but you can and should use this practice as one of the tactics to capturing her mind (refer to step #5).

10

Get Her Out Of Her Comfort Zone.

Most people don't understand that their family and friends are the very thing that is holding them back and keeping them from being successful or reaching their full potential. Most people get so comfortable that they become afraid of what is on the other side. This is the reason that most people will not cross the finish line on their own; they have to be pushed to their full potential.

Every professional athlete and successful business person had to go through this. All of them had someone that believed in them and saw their full potential even when they couldn't and pushed them to keep going and work harder and harder and study longer and longer and practice harder and harder. A major part of their success was their ability to dodge negative people that held them back, people that weren't an asset, people that were a distraction, etc. This is one reason why people move from their hometown after they reach a certain level of success. It is very important to get her out of her comfort zone (meaning location). But timing is the key. Do it at the right time.

11

Upgrade Her.

Meaning her mind, body and soul. I like to refer to this step as "lacing her". Regardless of if she is a quality woman or not you still should have the ability and the know how to turn a tramp into a champ. Give her a makeover, upgrade her clothes, and upgrade her mind frame. Raise her to enjoy being a woman to you and to honor and respect you as a man. Then after that, upgrade her car, upgrade her crib, her location, start a business with her, etc. Again, you actually have to do the shit then you will prove to her that you are like no other she has had and most likely will never meet again or very difficult to meet again. But this step is for upgrading her mind, body, and soul. The next step is for upgrading her living situation and status.

12

Get Her Stable And Established.

Going back to the previous step, this step is after you give her the makeover etc. And if she is already stable and established then you upgrade her current situation but only some time after you give her the makeover and she proves to you that she is qualified for all of this. Also it is important for you to understand that you should not get her fully stable and establish or upgrade her until her probation is over and you have made it official with her. Once you made it to step 12 her probation should be over. Steps 12, 13, 14, and 15 are for after the probation period. So make sure she is qualified.

(WARNING: DO NOT PUT CARS, HOUSES, OR A BUSINESS IN HER NAME! FIND A WAY AROUND DOING THIS. IF YOU DO THEN YOU ARE AT YOUR OWN RISK.)

13

Give Her Some Responsibilities To Make Her Feel Apart Of The Family Or Team.

If you are on something and are about your business, especially if you are capable of staying two steps ahead of her, leading her, upgrading her life, and giving her proper instructions (as well as doing any of the previous steps) then you can pull this one off naturally. Sometime around this step is when you should introduce her to the rest of her family or team if there is one. And if things are done right she will be excited and anxious to meet them. Maybe even nervous about if they would accept her or like her or if they are just as excited to meet her as she is to meet them. In other words, she is very optimistic and ready to continue to do her part to ensure you that the family gets ahead and stays ahead. If she is not at this point then you missed a step.

(Note: While I am at this step, it is important for me to let you know now that you will run across a lot of dominant women and passive aggressive women that although don't mind the whole family and team thing and working with other women, they do not want to live with them; which is a huge difference and prefer their own space.)

There is always something for her to do to help but she should be giving a particular role to play or a particular job title that is her responsibility to do and nobody else's. And make sure she understands the importance of it and make sure she is held accountable for it. And yes you will need to discipline her or them or sanction her or them at times in order to hold her or them accountable. We will get more into this in the next step. For now though, it is important to understand that if she does not feel a part of the big picture, if she does not feel a part of the team or family, then eventually she will leave and look for acceptance and appreciation somewhere else.

14

Find Appropriate Ways To Discipline Her Without Physical Abuse, Emotional Abuse, Or Verbal Abuse.

This step may be the most controversial out of all of the steps by far to a lot of people. I'm actually smiling on the inside of the thought of women's faces when they read this one. I can hear them now saying "what the fuck does he mean by discipline me" as well as a lot of negative comments and thoughts.

Yes ladies this step is crucial because if he does not know how to discipline you in an appropriate way then you will not maintain respect for him rather you are conscious of it or not. He would not be capable of leading you if he is not capable of disciplining/sanctioning you whenever it is appropriate. You may think it sounds crazy but you will allow him to discipline you when appropriate not because he "made you", but because of your respect for him. If you do not respect him enough then you will not allow it and you will leave him and you should leave him if you do not respect him.

However, fellas if you have been following these steps correctly then she should respect you by now without question. There should be no misunderstanding by now as to who is wearing the pants or panties. There is no doubt about who is the KING in her life and who her loyalty lies with. Fuck running your mouth about it and fuck her running her mouth about it. Talk is just talk. These steps require action and these steps demand realistic results. They all mean something. They all are part of the big picture. They all work but if you skip a step then it is a domino effect.

This step is a crucial and necessary step. You must learn to discipline her if you want to maintain her respect. PERIOD. Discipline is a part of leadership and you cannot have one without the other. So let's face it, who wants to be disciplined that doesn't have a fetish for it (and you have to watch out for this kind also because there is a huge community of people that get turned on by being "punished")? It's not meant to be fun or something that you like or enjoy so I can not think of anyone. So let me tell you now that none of the women will like it or want it and they damn sure don't want you to even think about disciplining them and they don't care about the reason for it. They don't want it, nobody wants it but it is necessary as a leader to know how to give sanctions. So that is why it is on this list. If you are too weak to lead her then leave her alone. Kings are Kings! Be the King she needs and not the sucker she wants!

Now that we have that understood, now we need to understand that it is by choice and not by force. You must learn to discipline her without physical abuse, emotional abuse, or verbal abuse (or disrespect). Everything is not the same for everyone and not all actions require the same disciplines, sanctions, or punishments. In other situations I am known to have her stand in the corner for a timeout for a certain amount of time. More serious situations I am known to "downgrade" her or remind her who she was before she met me. The final draw ultimately leads to me letting her go. Depending on the situation of course.

Oh yeah, and don't worry about her saying that she won't do it because if she doesn't then you just take it to the next level and let her weigh her options and give her her choices or ultimatum. One option is either she does it or she will lose the car or crib or business or all of the above if she doesn't respect you enough to do it. Another option is she loses all of the above including you if she doesn't do it. (Remember that you don't have anything in her name at this point. You are 2 steps ahead in this aspect and another reason why it is important to maintain leverage.) Trust me, despite her not wanting to do it after she weighs her options with your help she will pout and then stand in the corner because ultimately she would not only realize that what she will lose isn't worth it, but also it is her fault in the first place and you just cannot tolerate the disrespect. Physical abuse is never used and the only thing you will hurt is her pride and ego. If you have to get physical with her that means it is time to let her go, she isn't worth all of that energy to me.

15

Have A Realistic Retirement Plan For her Or With Her.

Last but not least, have a realistic retirement plan. Don't just sell her the dream champ, you have to "deliver" it also (which is easier said than done). You should retire when you have achieved all of your plans and goals.

Retirement does not mean quitting, the work never stops. Retiring means graduating to another level in life or elevating. You are just no longer doing the same things on the same level as you use too. You are not growing if you are not elevating. Once you guys have achieved your goals together then it is time to retire and you both should see and experience the obvious benefits together. Also, If you have not done it by this point, then it is ok to put the cars, cribs, businesses, etc. in her name (although I personally strongly advise you to not do this unless she proves to you that she deserves it).

DISCLAIMER: This list is intended to promote a long term healthy, positive, and productive relationship with a particular kind of lady and stay away from negativity, toxic, and counter productive people, situations, circumstances! What you eat does not make the other person shit and your dreams and happiness is not for others to understand. They should be worried about how to live their own dreams and achieve their own happiness.

About the Author

Jody Makc is an ex-pimp now entrepreneur, coach, and motivational speaker that reveals jaw dropping yet practical Business, Financial literacy, partnership/relationship to men. He is also the founder of the mighty Boss Player International, Inc. as well as the editor in chief of The Sauce Magazine (A lifestyle magazine for men with flavor). He was born in Jackson Mississippi and has lived most of his childhood in a small town call Vicksburg. Since then, he has been down and around throughout the United States minding his own business. When not conducting business, he can be found on the Las Vegas scene enjoying life and mastering himSELF one day at a time.

You can chat with or follow Jody Makc on Instagram at @jodymakc and @thesaucemag.
www.thesaucemagazine.com

In Memory Of

Breanna S White

Made in the USA
Middletown, DE
02 November 2022